Life is pure adventure, and the sooner we realize that, the quicker we will be able to treat life as art: to bring all our energies to each encounter. . .

— MAYA ANGELOU
FROM *WOULDN'T TAKE NOTHING FOR MY JOURNEY NOW*

MAYA ANGELOU

BY JUDITH E. HARPER

GRAPHIC DESIGN
Robert E. Bonaker / Graphic Design & Consulting Co.

PROJECT COORDINATOR
James R. Rothaus / James R. Rothaus & Associates

EDITORIAL DIRECTION
Elizabeth Sirimarco

COVER PHOTO
Portrait of Maya Angelou / AP Wide World Photos

Library of Congress Cataloging-in-Publication Data
Harper, Judith E.
Maya Angelou / by Judith E. Harper.
p. cm.
Summary: Examines the life and accomplishments of the
African American writer, performer, and teacher, as well
as her impact on literature and black culture.
ISBN 1-56766-570-5 (library reinforced : alk. paper)

1. Angelou, Maya — Juvenile literature. 2. Women authors,
American — 20th century — Biography — Juvenile literature.
3. Entertainers — United States — Biography — Juvenile
literature. 4. Afro-American women authors — Biography —
Juvenile literature.
[1. Angelou, Maya. 2. Authors, American. 3. Afro-Americans —
Biography. 4. Women — Biography] I. Title

PS3551.N464Z69 1999   98-45559
818'.5409 — dc21   CIP
[B]   AC

Contents

Early Life

When Maya Angelou was a 15-year-old high school student in San Francisco, California, she dreamed of working as a conductor on the city's streetcars. She was deeply disappointed when her mother told her, "They don't accept colored people on the streetcars." Sure enough, when Maya went to the office of the Market Street Railway Company, the receptionist refused to give her an application. She also dodged Maya's questions. Maya knew that this was *discrimination* — that she was denied the opportunity to apply for the job because she was African American.

The discrimination filled her with the fire and determination to get the job. Maya would not be turned away. Every day she returned to the company office to sit and wait for an application. Three weeks later, the company finally gave her an interview. She was hired, becoming the first African American to work on the streetcars of San Francisco. Overflowing with pride, Maya was thrilled by her victory. She knew now that she could achieve the things she wanted most in life.

In 1998, at age 70, Maya Angelou is considered one of the greatest writers in the United States. Her books and poems are admired all over the world. She has been a dancer, singer, songwriter, playwright, director, producer, teacher, writer, poet, and author, but her life has not been one huge success. Many times, even when she tried her hardest, she failed. Each time she found a way to keep on trying. Whenever Maya talks to young people today, she tells them what she most wants them to know. "You might encounter many defeats," she says, "but you must never be defeated."

UPI/Corbis-Bettmann

IN 1943, MAYA BECAME THE FIRST AFRICAN AMERICAN TO WORK ON THE FAMOUS STREETCARS OF SAN FRANCISCO.

UPI/Corbis-Bettmann

AFRICAN AMERICAN STUDENTS ATTEND AN ALL-BLACK SCHOOL. IN THE SOUTH, BLACK AND WHITE CHILDREN WERE NOT ALLOWED TO GO TO SCHOOL TOGETHER, AND SEGREGATION WAS A FACT OF SOUTHERN LIFE FOR MORE THAN HALF OF THE 20TH CENTURY.

Maya Angelou was born Marguerite Annie Johnson in St. Louis, Missouri, on April 4, 1928. Her brother Bailey Johnson was the first person to call her "Maya" when they were small children. In 1931, when Maya was three years old, she and four-year-old Bailey said good-bye to their parents and their home in Long Beach, California. Together they boarded a train for a four-day, cross-country journey — all on their own — to their grandmother in Stamps, Arkansas. Maya's parents had recently divorced, and their mother realized she could not earn a living and care for them, too. Maya and Bailey were bewildered by the move. They each thought that they had done something terribly wrong to cause their parents to send them away.

Their grandmother, Momma Henderson, was a kind but strict woman. She took good care of Maya and Bailey but did not show them much affection. As a deeply religious woman, she believed it was her duty to raise her grandchildren as devout, God-fearing Christians. Momma owned a small general store in Stamps, a tiny, poor country town. Although she had very little money, they did not go hungry as many White and African American people did during the Depression of the 1930s.

Stamps was very much like the rest of the southern United States at the time. It was *segregated*. African Americans lived in one section of town, and Whites lived in another. African Americans could attend only their own schools, buy food at their own stores, and worship at their own churches, although they were hired to work in White homes and businesses. If they were ill or dying, they could not be treated by a White doctor. If no Black doctors or nurses were available, they had to travel to another town to search for care or go without medical help.

Of all these problems, Maya has said that the White peoples' hatred of African Americans was the worst. Although there were exceptions, most White people in Stamps treated African Americans as if they were less than human. Some were merely unkind, while others were cruel. A few were even violent. *Lynchings*, the killings of African Americans by White mobs, were less common by the time of Maya's girlhood, but they still happened.

When Maya was very young, she seldom saw a White person. "Whitefolks" did not seem real to her. They were "strange pale creatures" whom she glimpsed only from afar. As she grew older and came into contact with the White people of Stamps, their unkindness made her angry. Fortunately, the Black community in Stamps was strong. Maya's neighbors supported and cared for one another in their dealings with White people. The stories and jokes they shared gave them the courage to face the constant *prejudice* and hatred.

UPI/Corbis-Bettmann

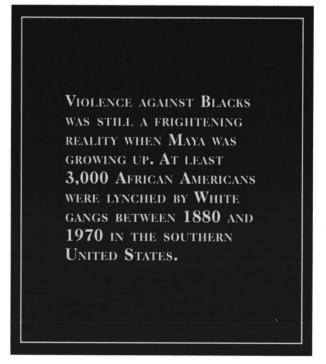

VIOLENCE AGAINST BLACKS WAS STILL A FRIGHTENING REALITY WHEN MAYA WAS GROWING UP. AT LEAST 3,000 AFRICAN AMERICANS WERE LYNCHED BY WHITE GANGS BETWEEN 1880 AND 1970 IN THE SOUTHERN UNITED STATES.

UPI/Corbis-Bettmann

IN 1922, THOUSANDS OF AFRICAN AMERICANS DEMONSTRATED IN WASHINGTON, D.C., AGAINST LYNCHINGS. VIOLENT CRIMES AGAINST BLACKS CONTINUED TO OCCUR IN THE DECADES THAT FOLLOWED.

Frank Capri/Archive Photos

THE DIFFICULT EXPERIENCES OF MAYA'S YOUTH
WOULD ONE DAY PLAY A ROLE IN HER SUCCESS
AS A WRITER.

Struggling to Survive

When Maya was seven years old, she made another long journey — this time to live with her mother in the city of St. Louis, Missouri. A year later, Maya suffered a severe *trauma*. Her mother's boyfriend *sexually abused* her when her mother was not at home. Afterward, Maya was terrified. She told no one because the man threatened to kill her brother Bailey if she did.

When her mother discovered the truth a few days later, she told the authorities, and the man was soon arrested. Maya testified at his trial, and he was sentenced to jail. He was murdered shortly after his early release from jail. Maya was horror-struck. She believed that if she had not spoken at the trial, he would still be alive. She became convinced that her voice was a murderous weapon, and she vowed not to speak again.

As the weeks passed, Maya's body healed, but her soul continued to suffer. Her determined silence disturbed her mother. After several months, her mother gave up trying to break through the wall that Maya had built up around herself. Her mother sent her and Bailey back to their grandmother in Arkansas. Momma Henderson and Bailey accepted and understood Maya's refusal to speak. Maya was grateful when Bailey tried to protect her from the hurtful comments of neighbors.

The period in which Maya was *mute* was a difficult one, but she learned a great deal from the experience. She kept her eyes wide open and observed the world around her carefully. She also lost herself in her reading. She not only read books, she devoured them. Maya especially loved the poetry of Shakespeare and of African American poet Paul Laurence Dunbar.

About one year after Maya returned to Arkansas, Bertha Flowers, the most educated Black woman in Stamps, invited Maya to her home. Maya was thrilled that this special woman noticed her. Miss Flowers read poetry to Maya and explained that the human voice is what fills words with meaning. She lent Maya a book of poetry and suggested she choose one to recite at their next visit. When Maya went home, she was walking on air. She felt special.

Through her friendship with Miss Flowers, Maya began to believe in herself. Eventually she started to speak, just a bit.

Maya was an excellent student all through grammar school. She graduated from the eighth grade at the top of her class. Momma noticed that Maya and Bailey were growing up fast. She told them that she was getting too old to care for them, and it was time that they live with their mother again. Maya always believed that another reason lay behind Momma's decision to send them back to their mother. Momma never said so, but Maya thinks that she was concerned about her grandchildren's future. Momma knew that they would have more opportunities and freedom in California than in the segregated South.

Corbis-Bettmann

THE WORK OF PAUL LAURENCE DUNBAR INSPIRED MAYA IN HER YOUTH. DUNBAR WAS THE FIRST AFRICAN AMERICAN POET TO RECEIVE NATIONAL RECOGNITION FROM WHITE AMERICANS.

Stephen Matteson, Jr./New York Times Co./Archive Photos

ALTHOUGH MAYA'S FIVE YEARS OF BEING MUTE WERE PAINFUL, SHE NOW BELIEVES THAT HER SILENCE TAUGHT HER MANY THINGS. SHE LEARNED HOW TO REALLY LISTEN. "I IMAGINED MY WHOLE BODY AS AN EAR," SHE SAID.

Maya was an achiever in high school, just as she had been in grammar school. She enjoyed studying dance and acting. She won a scholarship to the California Labor School, an evening college.

In 1945, a few months after she graduated from high school, Maya gave birth to a son, Clyde Bailey Johnson. She was 17 years old. She did not know the baby's father well, nor did she want to marry him. When her mother offered her the chance to live at home with her baby and attend college, Maya experienced a sudden surge of independence. Although she very much wanted to go to college, she felt an even stronger need to strike out on her own. She wanted to prove to herself and her family that she could support herself and her baby, so she rented a room and found a job as a cook.

A WHITE SEGREGATIONIST IN ARKANSAS TALKS TO A CROWD OF TEENAGERS IN THE 1960s. ARKANSAS WOULD REMAIN SEGREGATED FOR MANY YEARS AFTER MAYA LEFT THE SMALL TOWN OF STAMPS.

UPI/Corbis-Bettmann

A Difficult Road To Success

The next few years were a constant struggle. Maya worked as a cook and a waitress, all the time searching for good childcare for her baby. She moved from place to place and discovered how difficult life was for a single mother with a child to support.

For a brief time, Maya experimented with smoking marijuana. Just as she was thinking about trying other drugs, a close friend named Troubador Martin shocked her into stopping all her drug use. One day he explained to her how a dangerous drug called heroin was controlling and destroying his life. It was a lesson she would never forget. For this gift, she has always been grateful.

Maya realized she needed more support in her life. She moved in with her mother in San Francisco and found satisfying work in a music store.

Not long afterward, she married another music lover, Tosh Angelos, a Greek American. For a time, Maya enjoyed the security of having a husband and a home, but after two years of marriage, the lack of love in their relationship caused them to divorce.

Maya was then inspired to reach for a goal she had always dreamed of — to become a performer. While she was working as a waitress and dancer at a small club, the managers of a nightclub called The Purple Onion hired her as a singer and dancer of *calypso* music. Maya's act was a big hit. After talent scouts watched her perform, she was soon offered a role in an upcoming Broadway show.

A cover featuring Maya from a 1960 record album. In the 1950s, she had started using the name Maya Angelou (pronounced An-jeh-low). She arrived at the name "Angelou" by slightly changing her first husband's surname, Angelos.

Archive Photos

PORGY AND BESS, THE WELL-KNOWN AMERICAN OPERA, TELLS THE TRAGIC LOVE STORY OF AN AFRICAN AMERICAN MAN AND WOMAN THROUGH SONGS AND MUSIC.

On the same day she heard this good news, she was asked to be a leading dancer in a traveling company of artists performing *Porgy and Bess*, the great American opera. What triumph — to be able to choose between two outstanding roles! Maya had no trouble deciding which part to accept. She had always wanted to travel and to be a member of an all-Black theatrical company. In 1954, she joined the cast of *Porgy and Bess*.

With all this success came some pain. Since *Porgy and Bess* would tour 22 nations in Europe and Africa, she would not be able to take her son with her. Maya felt terrible leaving him at home with her mother. The separation was difficult for both Maya and her son. When Maya returned home many months later, she promised herself that she would not be separated from Guy (Clyde's new nickname for himself) again.

THE WHITE MUSICIAN GEORGE GERSHWIN, COMPOSER OF *PORGY AND BESS*, WAS SO FASCINATED BY AFRICAN AMERICAN JAZZ THAT IT INSPIRED ALL HIS MUSIC FOR THIS OPERA.

In 1959, Maya and Guy moved to New York City. She became involved in the African American community in the part of the city called Harlem. Maya knew she wanted to work as a writer. She joined the Harlem Writers Guild, a group of top-notch, hard-working African American writers.

Corbis-Bettmann

One day it was her turn to read her writing to the other members. When she finished reading a play she had written, one writer harshly criticized it. Maya was devastated. Just as she was planning to give up on writing, this same man spoke to her again. He explained that talent is not enough to become a writer. "You've got to work," he told her. "Write each sentence over and over again — and then write it again." Maya listened. She knew she had a hard road ahead of her if she wanted to be a writer, but she promised herself she would not quit.

UPI/Corbis-Bettmann

Genevieve Naylon/Corbis

"MAKING A DECISION TO WRITE," MAYA
HAS SAID, "WAS A LOT LIKE DECIDING
TO JUMP INTO A FROZEN LAKE. I KNEW
I WAS GOING IN."

Library of Congress/Corbis

BY THE 1950S, AFRICAN AMERICANS BEGAN TO PROTEST AGAINST SEGREGATION AND OTHER FORMS OF DISCRIMINATION.

The Civil Rights Movement

Harlem in the late 1950s was bursting with new life and hope. African Americans were protesting racial discrimination and prejudice. They were also joining *civil rights* workers who were opposing segregation in the South. It thrilled Maya to watch the *civil rights movement* gain in strength and power. Like many African Americans, Maya began to believe that equality was no longer an impossible dream, but a reality within their grasp.

After hearing the civil rights leader Martin Luther King, Jr. speak, Maya was determined to join his cause through his group the Southern Christian Leadership Conference (SCLC). With her friend Godfrey Cambridge, she gathered African American performers to appear in *Cabaret for Freedom*, a production that she created to raise money for the SCLC. It was enormously successful and also raised awareness about the civil rights struggle.

After this victory, she worked briefly as northern coordinator of the SCLC in 1960. During this exciting time, Maya met Vusumzi Make, a freedom fighter from South Africa. Make (pronounced Mah-kay), was traveling all over the world to gain support for his people's fight against *apartheid*. White South Africans created this policy of laws that denied Black South Africans of all their rights. Maya fell in love with Make and his fight to help his people. After a very brief courtship, they both agreed to consider their relationship a true marriage, although they never legally married.

One year later, she and Guy moved with Make to Cairo, Egypt. Maya was worried about the family's finances and also bored with the role of housewife. Though Make did not want her to work, Maya pursued a job as an editor at the *Arab Observer*, an English-language newspaper. Make was enraged when he found out. Didn't she know that African wives do only what their husbands want? Maya was sorry but knew that her need to be independent was more important than her wish to please him. In 1963, she left Make and moved with Guy to the city of Accra in Ghana.

Ghana was an exciting, colorful, newly independent nation in West Africa. Maya found a job working and teaching at the University of Ghana where Guy was a student. She also kept improving her writing by submitting articles to newspapers.

While in Ghana, Maya once again met Malcolm X, the *militant* African American leader. Years before, she had heard him speak in Harlem and had met with him about her civil rights activities. At that time, he was a key leader of the Nation of Islam, also known as the Black Muslims. He opposed Dr. King's strategy of nonviolence, the use of peaceful rather than violent methods to achieve civil rights. Malcolm X preached another, more radical message, "Freedom at any cost." Maya admired Malcolm X but did not agree with all his ideas.

Archive Photos

MALCOLM X GAVE AN ANGRY VOICE TO THE FRUSTRATION MANY BLACK AMERICANS FELT ABOUT RACISM AND PREJUDICE.

New York Times Co./Archive Photos

MAYA'S SOUTH AFRICAN HUSBAND, VUSUMZI MAKE, EXPECTED HER TO STOP WORKING AND STAY AT HOME, LIKE OTHER AFRICAN WIVES. INDEPENDENT AND STRONG, MAYA CHOSE INSTEAD TO CONTINUE HER GOAL OF BECOMING A SUCCESSFUL WRITER AND PURSUED A JOB WITH A NEWSPAPER CALLED THE *ARAB OBSERVER*.

SOLDIERS IN ACCARA, GHANA, RAISED THE NEW COUNTRY'S FLAG ON MARCH 6, 1957 — THE DAY GHANA BECAME AN INDEPENDENT NATION. GHANA WAS FORMERLY A BRITISH COLONY, CALLED THE GOLD COAST. SIX YEARS AFTER IT GAINED ITS INDEPENDENCE, MAYA AND HER SON MOVED THERE TO LIVE.

In Ghana, Maya discovered that Malcolm X had changed. He was no longer involved with the Nation of Islam, although he was still a devout Moslem. She was intrigued to hear him discuss his recent *pilgrimage* to Mecca, Saudi Arabia, the holiest city of *Islam*. While in Mecca, Malcolm's talks with Moslems from many nations caused him to rethink some of his ideas. He decided that he must work with White and Black leaders all over the world to achieve civil rights in the United States and independence for Blacks in Africa. He planned to convince African leaders of the United Nations to pressure the United States to give African Americans more civil rights.

Maya was inspired to help Malcolm X with his new mission, the Organization of Afro-American Unity (OAAU). He formed this group so that Africans, African Americans, and all people of African *ancestry* could work together to achieve human rights for people throughout the world. He hired Maya to serve as a coordinator of the OAAU. She was to begin this new job as soon as she returned to the United States. Two days after she arrived in the United States, on February 21, 1965, Malcolm X was *assassinated*. Maya was in anguish over his death. She grieved for him and for their cause. After the assasination, she supported the civil rights movement as much as ever but decided that she would no longer play such an active role within it.

NO ONE KNOWS FOR SURE WHO KILLED MALCOLM X. SOME PEOPLE BELIEVE THAT LEADERS OF THE NATION OF ISLAM HAD HIM ASSASSINATED; OTHERS BELIEVE THAT THE U.S. GOVERNMENT MAY HAVE BEEN INVOLVED.

Fulfillment

In the late 1960s, Maya focused her energies on her writing. In 1970, her book *I Know Why the Caged Bird Sings* was published. This first volume of her autobiography told the story of her childhood. It became an immediate bestseller and was nominated for the National Book Award.

During the 1970s and 1980s, Maya worked intently and had more success than ever before. She wrote and published four more volumes of her autobiography and several books of poetry. In 1972, she was nominated for a Pulitzer Prize for her first published book of verse, *Just Give Me a Cool Drink of Water 'fore I Diiie*. When she wrote the script for the movie *Georgia, Georgia* in 1972, she became the first African American woman to have a screenplay produced in Hollywood. In 1977, she appeared in one of the most popular television miniseries of all time. Written by Alex Haley, *Roots* told the true story of an African American family's journey from slavery to freedom. She was nominated for an Emmy Award for her performance. In 1981, she was selected to be the Reynolds Professor of American Studies at Wake Forest University in Winston-Salem, North Carolina, where she continues to work and live today.

When President-Elect Bill Clinton was planning his 1993 inauguration, he asked Maya to compose and recite a special poem at the ceremony. She was deeply honored. Before she finished the poem, she covered more than two hundred pages with writing! On January 21, 1993, she read "On the Pulse of Morning" to millions of Americans.

AP Wide World Photos

MAYA'S FIRST BOOK, *I KNOW WHY THE CAGED BIRD SINGS*, WAS PUBLISHED IN **1970.**

AP Wide World Photos

MAYA POSES WITH THE PRESIDENT OF SPELMAN COLLEGE,
JOHNETTA COLE, AT THE EIGHTH BLACK HISTORY MAKERS
AWARDS. MAYA RECEIVED THIS AWARD IN 1994.

In the late 1990s, Maya is still writing. When she is at work, she allows no distractions to disturb her. She gets out of bed at about 5 AM and takes a shower. She then drives to a hotel room and starts working by 6:30, with the Bible and *Roget's Thesaurus* by her side. She writes until 12:30 PM, at which time she tears herself away to return home to other activities. Still her writing day is not over. In the evening she edits what she has written that morning. "So if I've written 10 or 12 pages in six hours," Maya says, "it'll end up as three or four if I'm lucky." She admits that even though she must overcome her fear of writing every single day, it is the most important and fulfilling part of her life.

Maya feels a special closeness to children. In December 1996, she was appointed a National Ambassador for the United Nations International Children's Emergency Fund (UNICEF). In this role, she alerts Americans to the importance of UNICEF's work while also helping raise money to aid children in need around the world.

YOUNG DIRECTOR JOHN SINGLETON ASKED MAYA TO WRITE THE POETRY FOR HIS MOVIE, *POETIC JUSTICE*, A STORY ABOUT AN AFRICAN AMERICAN POET.

Archive Photos

Since reading helped Maya to survive her childhood and to reach out for what she most wanted in her life, she spreads the message that books are power. She believes that reading *empowers* children to work toward their most treasured goals. She also hopes that her work as a literacy activist will help to eliminate *illiteracy*.

Maya is also an accomplished *orator*. Nearly everywhere she speaks, she finds a way to tell people that courage is the human quality she admires most. She also wants to make sure people understand what she means by courage. "It doesn't mean not being afraid," she says. "It means being afraid but facing it."

Maya Angelou has spent a lifetime facing her fears, pushing through them, rising above them, and never giving up. Although she has enjoyed all her successes, she admits that her failures have also been useful. "Each time you overcome a burden or a barrier," she says, "you feel better about yourself. You become stronger." Thanks to Maya's courage, she has been strong enough to keep giving the precious gift of herself — through the art of her books and poetry.

AP Wide World Photos

MAYA TRAVELS GREAT DISTANCES TO DELIVER LECTURES ABOUT HER LIFE AND HER WRITINGS AS WELL AS TO RECITE HER POETRY.

AP Wide World Photos

PRESIDENT BILL CLINTON REACHED OUT TO EMBRACE MAYA AFTER SHE READ HER POEM, "ON THE PULSE OF MORNING," FOR HIS 1993 INNAUGURATION.

AP Wide World Photos

Timeline

1928   Marguerite Annie Johnson is born in St. Louis, Missouri, on April 4.

1943   Marguerite becomes the first African American streetcar conductor in San Francisco.

1945   Marguerite graduates from high school in San Francisco and gives birth to her son, Clyde Bailey "Guy" Johnson.

1953   Marguerite lands a job singing and dancing at The Purple Onion, a San Francisco nightclub, and begins using the name Maya Angelou.

1954   Maya joins the cast of *Porgy and Bess* and has the opportunity to travel to 22 nations in Europe and Africa.

1959   Maya moves to New York with Guy and joins the Harlem Writers Guild.

1960   Maya meets Martin Luther King, Jr. She forms a close relationship with Vusumzi Make, a South African freedom fighter.

1961   Maya moves to Cairo, Egypt, with Vusumzi Make and Guy.

1963   Maya and Guy move to Accra, Ghana.

1965   Maya returns to the United States and learns of the assassination of Malcolm X.

1970   *I Know Why the Caged Bird Sings* is published.

1972   Maya becomes the first African American woman to have a screenplay produced in Hollywood.

1977   Maya is nominated for an Emmy Award for her performance in the television miniseries *Roots*.

1993   President Bill Clinton askes Maya to recite one of her poems at his inauguration.

1996   UNICEF appoints Maya as a National Ambassador.

1998   Maya celebrates her 70th birthday.

Glossary

ancestry
An individual's ancestors; a person of African ancestry has one or more ancestors who originated in Africa.

apartheid
The former official policy of segregation and discrimination established by the government of the Republic of South Africa. This policy was finally eliminated in 1991.

assassinate
To murder a prominent individual, usually a leader in politics or in government.

calypso
A type of music from the West Indies with a lively rhythm and beat.

civil rights
The personal freedoms belonging to all citizens of the United States as guaranteed by the Constitution and its ammendments.

civil rights movement
The protests and political action of African American and White activists who worked to achieve civil rights and equality for minorities during the 1950s and 1960s.

discrimination
Different treatment of a person or people because of race, religion, nationality, sex, or group.

empower
To give power or courage.

illiteracy
The inability to read and write.

Islam
The religion practiced by Moslems, followers of Mohammed.

lynching
A murder that is carried out by a mob of people.

militant
Supporting the solution of problems by violent means; aggressive.

mute
Unable to speak; being silent or without speech.

orator
A highly skilled public speaker.

pilgrimage
A journey to a sacred place.

prejudice
A bad feeling or opinion about something or someone without just reason; feeling anger toward a group or its characteristics.

segregate
To separate or isolate people into groups, often according to race.

sexually abuse
To harm or injure another person by inappropriately touching or making contact with his or her sexual organs.

trauma
A severe injury to the body or to the mind, often with harmful, long-lasting effects.

Index

For Further Information

Angelou, Maya. *I Know Why the Caged Bird Sings*. New York, NY: Random House. 1970 (adult title).

Dunn, John M. *The Civil Rights Movement*. World History Series. San Diego, CA: Lucent Books, 1998.

King, Sarah E. *Maya Angelou: Greeting the Morning*. Brookfield, CT: Millbrook Press, 1994.

Shapiro, Miles. *Maya Angelou*. Black Americans of Achievement Series. New York, NY: Chelsea House Publishers, 1994.

Shuker, Nancy. *Maya Angelou*. Genius! The Artist and the Process Series. Englewood Cliffs, NJ: Silver Burdett Press. 1990.

Weisbrot, Robert. *Marching Toward Freedom 1957-1965*. Milestones in Black American History Series. New York, NY: Chelsea House. 1994.

Web Sites
http://ucaswww.mcm.uc.edu/worldfest/about.html
http://www.mojones.com/mother_jones/MJ95/kelley.html

Sources of Quoted Material

p. 6: "They don't accept..." *I Know Why the Caged Bird Sings*. Bantam,1993. p. 225. "You might encounter..." "A Conversation with Maya Angelou" by Bill Moyers, broadcast on WNET November, 21, 1973. Reprinted in *Conversations with Maya Angelou*, p. 24.

p. 10: "Whitefolks"... "strange pale creatures." *I Know Why the Caged Bird Sings*, pp.20-21.

p. 16: "I imagined my whole body..." from "How Maya Angelou Overcame All the Odds" by Bev Gilligan, first published in *Woman Magazine*, reprinted in *Conversations*, p. 203.

p. 22: "You've got to work..." *The Heart of a Woman*. Bantam, 1997. p. 44.

p. 23: "Making a decision..." *The Heart of a Woman*, p. 48.

p. 33: "So if I've written..." from "A Life in the Day of Maya Angelou." by Carol Sarler. *The Sunday Times Magazine*. December 17, 1987. Reprinted in *Conversations,* pp. 216-217.

p. 34: "It doesn't mean not being afraid..." by Bev Gilligan, first published in *Woman Magazine*, reprinted in *Conversations*, p. 203. "Each time you overcome a burden..." from "Singing, Swinging, and Still Living Life to the Full" by Devinia Sookia in *Caribbean Times*, August 21, 1987. Reprinted in *Conversations*, p. 192.